CRAZY CREATURES OF THE ANIMAL KINGDOM

WHAT DO YOU KNOW ABOUT ALBINO ANIMALS?

FRANCINE TOPACIO

PowerKiDS press
New York

Published in 2021 by The Rosen Publishing Group, Inc.
29 East 21st Street, New York, NY 10010

First Edition

Portions of this work were originally authored by Marie Racanelli and published as *Albino Animals*. All new material this edition authored by Francine Topacio.

Editor: Kara Murray
Book Design: Tanya Dellaccio

Photo Credits: Cover R. Andrew Odum/Photodisc/Getty Images; p. 4 Mark Kostich/iStock/Getty Images; p. 5 Coatesy/Shutterstock.com; p. 7 Christine Bird/Shutterstock.com; p. 9 Vladimir Wrangel/Shutterstock.com; p. 11 (salamander) Jay Ondreicka/Shutterstock.com; p. 11 (kitten) Dora Zett/Shutterstock.com; p. 12 Portland Press Herald/Getty Images; p. 14 Tanasut Chindasuthi/Shutterstock.com; p. 15 Artush/Shutterstock.com; p. 17 Fernando Camino/Getty Images; p. 19 (alligator) You Touch Pix of EuToch/Shutterstock.com; p. 19 (cobra) Akarat Duangkhong/Shutterstock.com; p. 21 Tony Campbell/Shutterstock.com; p. 22 StockPhotosArt/Shutterstock.com.

Library of Congress Cataloging-in-Publication Data

Names: Topacio, Francine, author.
Title: What do you know about albino animals? / Francine Topacio.
Description: New York : PowerKids Press, [2021] | Series: Crazy creatures of the animal kingdom | Includes index.
Identifiers: LCCN 2019051798 | ISBN 9781725319646 (paperback) | ISBN 9781725319660 (library binding) | ISBN 9781725319653 (6 pack)
Subjects: LCSH: Albinos and albinism—Juvenile literature. | Animal pigments—Juvenile literature.
Classification: LCC RL790 .T67 2021 | DDC 616.5/5–dc23
LC record available at https://lccn.loc.gov/2019051798

Manufactured in the United States of America

CPSIA Compliance Information: Batch #CSPK20. For Further Information contact Rosen Publishing, New York, New York at 1-800-237-9932.

CONTENTS

WHITE AND PINK ALL OVER

Animals come in all the colors of the rainbow and more! Sometimes, though, an animal may be born with different coloring from other animals like it. Some animals are born with white fur or skin and pink eyes. These animals are albinos.

If a tree frog is born with albinism, how does it differ from a tree frog that is green? In most ways, the two frogs don't differ at all. They eat the same foods. They're both about the same size. They even make the same sounds. The key difference is that the albino frog's body doesn't make a **pigment** called **melanin**.

ALBINO TREE FROG

This albino hedgehog eats the same insects, worms, and fruit that any other hedgehog might be looking to eat.

MELANIN IN OUR WORLD

Pigments bring color to our world. Leaves are green and flamingos are pink because of pigments. Melanin is the pigment that produces colors in skin, hair, and eyes. Animals with albinism don't make melanin. When this pigment is missing, it leads to the lack of color in animals' skin, hair, feathers, fur, **scales**, and eyes. Albino animals' eyes appear pink because their blood vessels can be seen in the eyes. In animals without albinism, these blood vessels would be hidden by melanin.

Animals are born with albinism. It's in their **genes**. This means it's a **disorder** that's passed down from their parents. It can't be cured or outgrown.

HOW STRANGE!

You're more likely to spot albino **mammals** than other kinds of albino animals. This is because the only pigment mammals' bodies produce is melanin. Other animals produce multiple kinds of pigments.

Squirrels can be many colors, including black, gray, red, brown, or white. You can tell this squirrel is albino, though, because of its red eyes.

IS IT A TRUE ALBINO?

Did you know that not all white animals are albinos? To tell if an animal is albino, you need to look at its eyes. The lack of melanin produces eyes that look pinkish red or blue. This is the eye color of a true albino. White animals that have regular coloring in their eyes are called **leucistic**. These animals have less of all skin pigments, not just melanin.

Some animals, like the polar bear or snowy owl, have white fur or feathers, but they aren't albino or leucistic. Their bodies produce pigments, but they have adapted, or changed over time, to having white coverings because it helps them live in their snow-covered homes.

HOW STRANGE!

Some zoos and wild animal breeders have bred lions to produce more white young since their color is so beautiful. This has caused many problems for the animals though.

White lions, like this one, are leucistic, not albino. You can tell because its eyes aren't red and its fur and skin have some color.

ALBINOS WITH SOME COLOR

In most albino animals, the fur, feathers, or scales are white, and the eyes are pink or pale blue. Some animals' bodies, though, make pigments other than melanin. Since albinism affects only melanin, this means that these animals can have color from these other pigments.

In a few cases, some albino animals may begin to show some color as they grow older. This can happen if the animal produces very small amounts of melanin.

Some animals produce melanin in certain parts of their bodies, such as their tails or their ear tips, but not in other parts. These animals are called partial albinos.

This albino salamander appears more yellow than white. This is because most amphibians' bodies produce pigments other than melanin.

HOW STRANGE!

Siamese cats are a special kind of partial albino animal. They are called temperature-**sensitive** albinos. This means the cooler parts of their bodies appear dark, while the warmer parts appear lighter.

ALL ABOUT ALBINOS

1 Albino animals have pinkish-red eyes. This is how you tell they're albino!

2 The chances of an albino lobster being born is 1 in 100 million.

3 There are likely only about 100 albino alligators alive in the world today. Most of them live in zoos.

4 When two parents carry the **recessive** gene that causes albinism, there's still only a 1 in 4 chance the baby will be born an albino.

5 Zookeepers sometimes put sunscreen on albino kangaroos so they won't get sunburned.

6 In the United States, about 1 in 20,000 people is born with albinism. In other parts of the world, however, it's more common. In some areas, about 1 in 1,000 babies can be born with albinism.

7 People with albinism often face discrimination in their communities. Sometimes kids with albinism are bullied.

8 Even plants can be white, but this is almost always deadly for them. If a plant lacks chlorophyll, which is a green chemical in its leaves that it needs to make food from sunlight, it can't live once it uses up the stored food in its seed.

ALBINO EYES

Albino animals have poor eyesight. This is due to the lack of melanin in their eyes. Melanin helps the eyes develop normally. With little or no melanin, an albino animal's eyes can't see the things a healthy animal's eyes can. While albinos aren't totally blind, they can't see very well. Their eyes often can't focus well or see how far away something is.

Melanin also gives the eye's iris its color. When there's no melanin, blood vessels show through the iris. That's why the eyes of an albino animal usually appear to be pinkish red. Sometimes, because of the way light shines into the iris, the eyes look pale blue.

The red eyes of the wallaby on the left tell us that it's an albino. In the wild, this wallaby would face dangers due to how it stands out.

ALL SHAPES AND SIZES

Albinism occurs in nearly every kind of animal all over the world. It's seen in mammals, reptiles, amphibians, fish, birds, and shellfish. From snails to squirrels and from people to whales, albinos can be found among all of them.

People are often interested in seeing albino animals. Over the years, some of these animals have become well known in zoos. One famous albino animal was a gorilla named Snowflake. He was born in Africa. In 1966, he was caught, and he lived for nearly 40 years in the Barcelona Zoo, in Spain. Many people came to see Snowflake. It was a sad day when he died of skin cancer in 2003.

Snowflake was the only known albino western lowland gorilla. Scientists studied him and his genes a great deal to learn more about albinism.

THE HARD LIVES OF ALBINO ANIMALS

In the natural world, there are often **predators** all around. It's hard for albino animals to hide from them. Albino animals' white bodies and poor eyesight make them easy to hunt. These things also make it hard for albino predators to hunt well. They can't easily see their **prey**, and the prey can see them coming. Albino animals also aren't often picked as mates because they look so different.

Snakes, frogs, and alligators need sunlight to keep warm. Because they have no melanin, though, albino animals' skin is very sensitive to the effects of sunlight. They sunburn easily. The sun hurts their bodies instead of helping them.

HOW STRANGE!

Scientists think albino alligators can't survive even a day in the wild. They are likely to be eaten by other predators, and their bodies can be hurt badly by the sun.

As fierce as this albino king cobra looks, it likely has trouble as a hunter. Since its eyes have trouble judging distance, that makes it hard to make a successful kill.

THE SPECIAL SQUIRRELS OF OLNEY, ILLINOIS

Olney, Illinois, is a special city. It's not for a reason you might expect, though! Olney is home to about 60 albino squirrels. Each fall, people count the squirrels to see if their numbers have changed.

Special laws in Olney **protect** the squirrels. If a squirrel is in the street, cars have to stop so the squirrel can pass. Dogs and cats aren't allowed to run loose because they might hurt the squirrels. Police officers in Olney even have an image of an albino squirrel on their arm patch. The number of albino squirrels in Olney has gone down in recent years, but the community is dedicated to keeping them safe.

HOW STRANGE!

Brevard, North Carolina, holds an annual White Squirrel Festival. The festival celebrates the town's large population of leucistic squirrels.

Albino squirrels are easy targets for predators, including cats and hawks, since they stand out against trees and grass. Olney works hard to protect their special squirrels!

HOW RARE ARE ALBINO ANIMALS?

For an albino animal to be born, each parent must carry the recessive gene that causes albinism. If only one has it, then the animal won't be albino. If two animals with that recessive gene have babies together, the chances are only one in four that they will have an albino baby. That is why albinism, in general, is so rare.

When albinism does occur in the wild, the animals have a small chance of staying alive. They have a better chance in zoos, where people take care of them. Albino animals are a rare and beautiful sight. Maybe you will spot one some day!

GLOSSARY

disorder: A sickness or medical condition.

gene: A tiny part of a living cell. Genes tell your cells how your body will look and act.

leucistic: Having to do with a disorder in which the body doesn't make any pigments.

mammal: Any warm-blooded animal whose babies drink milk and whose body is covered with hair or fur.

melanin: The dark pigment that determines the color in skin, hair, fur, feathers, scales, and eyes.

pigment: Matter that gives color.

predator: An animal that kills other animals for food.

prey: An animal that is hunted by another animal for food.

protect: To keep safe.

recessive: Having to do with a gene that doesn't give traits unless there are two present.

scale: One of many small, thin, plates that cover the bodies of snakes, lizards, other reptiles, and many fish.

sensitive: Easily harmed or damaged by certain conditions.

INDEX

WEBSITES

Due to the changing nature of Internet links, PowerKids Press has developed an online list of websites related to the subject of this book. This site is updated regularly. Please use this link to access the list: www.powerkidslinks.com/ccofak/albino